My First Day at School

by **Thomas Kingsley Troupe**

illustrated by **Kat Uno**

PICTURE WINDOW BOOKS
a capstone imprint

Halima

Name: **Halima**

Birthday: **June 22**

Favorite color: **purple**

Favorite food: **pizza**

Favorite animal: **horse**

I want to be a: **chef**

Table of Contents

The First, First Day. 4

Saying Goodbye. 6

Finding My Spot. 8

Bathroom Rules 10

Songs and Stories 12

Hands-on Fun 14

Fresh Air and Food 16

Learn and Play. 18

Time to Go Already? 20

Glossary. 22

Read More 23

Internet Sites. 23

Critical Thinking Questions 23

Index. 24

The First, First Day

Hi, my name is Halima. See me with my mom and dad? Have you been to school yet? I didn't know *what* to think on my first day. I didn't know any of the kids or teachers. There were new rules to learn. But everything went great! You might be a little worried about school too. That's OK! Let me tell you about my first day.

Saying Goodbye

Mom and Dad walked me to school that morning. I saw other kindergartners like me. A couple kids were crying. They didn't want their parents to leave. I didn't want mine to leave either, but I knew they would be back.

My teacher, Ms. Sara, had a nice smile. She lined us up and led us to our classroom.

Finding My Spot

First Ms. Sara showed us our lockers. We put our jackets, backpacks, and extra clothes in them. I learned not to slam the door shut. No one wants pinched fingers!

Next Ms. Sara asked us to find our spot in the classroom. My chair was next to a girl named Olivia. I told her I liked her name. She said she liked mine too! Peter and Malcolm were our other two table friends.

Oli

Halima

YOUR TURN! What kinds of things do you bring to school and where do you keep them?

Bathroom Rules

After a little while, we had our first bathroom break. Ms. Sara said we should all try to go to the bathroom during the break. If we had to go at another time, we should raise our hand and tell her. She showed us how to wash our hands when we were done too. We do a "one-two." That's one squirt of soap and two paper towels.

A girl named Avery had an accident later, before lunch. "That's OK," Ms. Sara said. "Accidents happen!" She got Avery cleaned up and helped her put on the extra pants she had in her locker.

Songs and Stories

Ms. Sara wanted us to get to know each other. So we took turns saying our names. We shared what we did over the summer. Some kids were shy. They didn't want to talk. But Ms. Sara smiled and asked them a few questions. Then they felt better. I told a funny story about my dog.

YOUR TURN! What summer story would you share with your class?

12

Ms. Sara taught us a silly song. We didn't use our quiet voices either. We were *loud!*

At story time. Ms. Sara read to us. She's a good reader. I want to be a good reader someday too.

YOUR TURN! What is your favorite book? How would you tell the story to a friend?

Hands-on Fun

The rest of the morning, we did all kinds of stuff. Table One played with clay. Table Two did puzzles. Table Three sat with Ms. Sara to practice writing our names. We switched tables after a while.

Olivia and I worked with Ms. Sara first. We wrote our names and colored around them. I only broke two crayons!

Fresh Air and Food

It was almost time for lunch. I smelled chicken nuggets! But first my class had recess. We grabbed our jackets and went outside to play. Ms. Sara told us to take turns so everyone could have fun. I went on the swings with Olivia. She made her swing go high!

YOUR TURN! What do you like to do at recess?

16

Swinging made me hungry. Ms. Sara led us to the lunchroom and showed us how to get our food. She showed us where to sit too. Some kids brought food from home. I got my very own tray and ate *all* of my lunch. When we were done, Ms. Sara helped us recycle our trash.

Learn and Play

After lunch we did flash cards. We learned about numbers, colors, and the ABCs. Ms. Sara told us we did a great job and gave us free-choice time. We could pick what we wanted to do. Some kids looked at books. Others played music or built things. Olivia and I painted.

When free-choice time was done, we all helped clean up. We put things back where they belonged.

Time to Go Already?

Ms. Sara pointed to the clock. "It's almost time to go home!" she said. "Already?" I asked. All of us got our jackets and backpacks from our lockers. But Ms. Sara had one more thing to teach us. The goodbye song!

My parents were waiting for me outside. They had so many questions. I couldn't wait to tell them about Ms. Sara, my new friends, and my first day at school!

Glossary

accident—when something happens quickly and by mistake

choice—something that is picked from a number of other things

locker—a small space to store and keep things safe

pinched—squeezed tightly between two things

practice—to keep working to get better at a skill

recess—a break from schoolwork, usually outside

recycle—to sort used items that can later be made into new products; paper, plastic, and glass are often recycled

squirt—a little bit of liquid

switch—to change one thing for another

Read More

Butterfield, Moira. *Schools Around the World.* Children Like Us. New York: Cavendish Square, 2016.

O'Connell, Eleanor. *Schools Around the World.* Adventures in Culture. New York: Gareth Stevens Publishing, 2017.

Smith, Penny. *A School Like Mine: A Celebration of Schools Around the World.* Children Just Like Me. New York: DK Publishing, 2016.

Internet Sites

Use FactHound to find Internet sites related to this book.

Visit *www.facthound.com*

Just type in 9781515838470 and go.

Critical Thinking Questions

1. Think about Halima's first day at school. What parts of your first day are you most looking forward to and why?

2. What kinds of things did Halima learn on her first day at school?

3. Do you think Halima made a friend on her first day at school? Use the text and illustrations to support your answer.

Index

bathrooms, 10

free-choice time, 18

learning, 18

lockers, 8, 11, 20

lunch, 16, 17, 18

names, 9, 12, 14, 15

parents, 4, 6, 21

recess, 16

songs, 13, 20

stories, 12, 13

Look for all the books in the series:

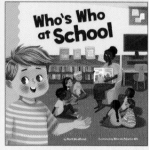

Special thanks to our adviser, Sara Hjelmeland, M.Ed., Kindergarten Teacher, for her expertise.

Editor: Jill Kalz
Designer: Lori Bye
Production Specialist: Laura Manthe
The illustrations in this book were created digitally.

Picture Window Books are published by Capstone
1710 Roe Crest Drive, North Mankato, Minnesota 56003
www.mycapstone.com

Library of Congress Cataloging-in-Publication Data is available on the Library of Congress website.
ISBN 978-1-5158-3847-0 (library binding)
ISBN 978-1-5158-4062-6 (paperback)
ISBN 978-1-5158-3853-1 (eBook PDF)
Summary: What's the first day of kindergarten like? Covering all the basics, from lockers and bathroom etiquette to playground rules and lunchtime, *My First Day of School* walks young readers through a typical first, first day of school, complete with kid-friendly, 1st-person narration and playful yet realistic illustrations that embrace diversity.

Shutterstock: jannoon028, (notebook) design element throughout

Printed in the United States of America.
PA49